EDUCATIONAL VALUES
A Seminar Report

Edited by

Peter Jones

Institute Occasional Papers 5

A Seminar Report based on the meeting held in
The University of Edinburgh,
29th - 30th April 1994,
by
The Institute for Advanced Studies in the Humanities

EDINBURGH: 1994

First Published 1994

ISBN 0 9514854 5 8

TABLE OF CONTENTS

Introduction

The Institute project, **Costing Values**, has three goals:

1. to identify and analyse fundamental ideas on which everyday decisions rest, throughout the world, but which never receive such attention;

2. to bring together from different walks of life the very people who make the daily decisions and need to reflect on such ideas - leaders from industry, commerce, politics, the diplomatic world, as well as from specialist professions and research institutes;

3. to challenge and transcend the boundaries of current thinking by insisting on perspectives from different cultures.

An Institute seminar held in Edinburgh in May 1993, under the title **Indigenous Peoples and Ethnic Minorities**, focussed on the disparities between races and cultures, and the implications of those disparities. Questions arose of human rights and of minorities, of multi-culturalism and of identity, of principles and practice. Some of these issues arose again in the Institute meeting opened by the President of Malta, in Valletta, in December 1993. That meeting, held under the title **Family Values in the Mediterranean**, heard presentations from a variety of perspectives. The seminar focussed on three main issues. First: everyone agreed that, in the context of

1

ever-present and rapid change, it is essential to identify precisely what is changing, under what conditions, at what rates, and within what domains. Second: detailed regional presentations from Malta itself, USA, UK, Israel, Egypt, Tunisia, Greece, Morrocco, Italy and France underlined important similarities and dissimilarities throughout the region. Thirdly, some attempt was made to formulate recommendations for social policy in the different regions, and to identify the most urgent practical and theoretical issues requiring analysis.

The Edinburgh Meeting on **Educational Values**, in April 1994, considered the rapidly changing views about education throughout the world, as well as the resources necessary to implement evolving ideas. It was acknowledged that many central questions about education remain unresolved. For example, there is no agreement on the best ages and stages for acquiring different skills and frames of mind in different cultures, and there is no agreement on all the factors that need to be monitored to ensure sustained motivation and the willingness to change.

Sir John Cassels, who opened the seminar, is Director of the National Commission on Education; Professor John Howie, author of the report *Upper Secondary Education in Scotland*, is Regius Professor of Mathematics in the University of St. Andrews; Senator

Victoria Camps, formerly Professor of Moral and Political Philosophy in the Autonomous University of Barcelona, is a Senator of the Spanish Parliament; Sir John Thomson was formerly UK Permanent Representative at the United Nations; Senator Masao Kunihiro is a member of the House of Councillors in Tokyo and was formerly Professor of Anthropology at Tokyo International University and Sophia University.

I am most grateful to the speakers for permission to edit texts based on their presentations, and also to the Chairmen of the seminar: Professor Jack Shaw, Chairman of the Scottish Higher Education Funding Council; Sir Kenneth Alexander, Chancellor of the University of Aberdeen; and Sir Mark Russell, former UK Ambassador to Turkey.

Synopsis

1. Knowledge is now accepted as an essential component of economic success. Societies which lack knowledge-based skills will be unable to compete, and will risk high levels of unemployment, and a likely collapse of social cohesion.

2. The British education system has important strengths, particularly at the University level, but also serious weaknesses lower down. In 1993 almost 20% of school leavers in Britain were found to be illiterate or innumerate or both. Too few young people stay in school till 18. Lack of motivation is widespread, partly because what is taught is perceived by pupils themselves to be irrelevant to real life.

3. There is a need for:
    a) much greater emphasis on vocational training and education;
    b) raising of the school leaving age to 18;
    c) education to be understood and presented as a continuing process through life;
    d) much less emphasis placed on a first degree taken immediately after leaving school.

4.   To provide the resources for improved primary and secondary education, money will have to come from tertiary education, chiefly through students paying a much higher proportion of their own expenses.

5.   Within the secondary system in the U.K. there is a sharp contrast between the narrow but deep 'A' level system of England and the much wider curriculum embraced by the Baccalauréat in France. Scottish Highers stand somewhere in between, but provide neither the high standards of 'A' levels nor the breadth of the French system.

6.   The English and French systems each have advantages and disadvantages. But the extreme specialisation at an early age required by 'A' levels must be wrong in an era where adaptability, language skills, numeracy, literacy and an understanding of our complex histories are all important.

7.   A narrowly utilitarian and vocational approach to education is inadequate. Education must not only prepare people for life but continue to help them during their lives; it must provide a moral and ethical input as well as one targetted at efficiency. Technologists must be aware of the wider implications of their contributions, and there must be room

for pure as well as applied science. The humanities likewise are a vital component in any balanced educational system. The traditional compartments of enquiry may have increased focus and efficiency in the past, but can be obstacles to educational reform, and mutual understanding.

8.   Globally, education must be seen within a context of democratic values, fairness, competitiveness and the growing interdependence of different areas of the world. In a rapidly developing and increasingly complex world, education, paradoxically, may have to become in one sense more basic. People must learn how to learn, in order to cope with the changes which will occur during their lives. At the same time more elements of compulsion may be needed: children cannot be allowed to leave school having achieved nothing: and in countries where women are severely educationally disadvantaged radical changes are necessary. But it is an open question whether the liberal Western values have universal validity. Some societies, e.g. notably China, place much greater emphasis on collective rather than individual good. Education in its widest sense will face severe challenges in meeting the requirements of a world which is growing closer together while retaining very wide disparities of outlook and achievement.

9.   Turning from a European to a Far Eastern perspective,
       Japan has been held up as a model of economic progress,
       much of which is attributed to the success of Japanese
       education. Japan has had a tradition of high literacy and
       numeracy, which has enabled its population to adjust
       rapidly to the needs of an industrial and technological age.
       But while Japanese education has enormous strengths in
       terms of providing its pupils with qualifications, through the
       assimilation of facts and knowledge, it is far weaker in
       terms of creativity and the encouragement of thought. It is
       in many respects the reverse of the British coin.

10.   No single system of education has the solution to all the
       current challenges. The needs of the economy exert political
       and social pressures which education must itself be strong
       enough to absorb and supplement, ensuring that values are
       identified, instigated and upheld. A notion of the
       humanities traceable to Cicero would celebrate both the
       utilitarian justification of all enquiry, but also the need to
       resist attempts to fragment enquiry and exclude interlopers.
       The motivation of all citizens will crucially depend on the
       success with which education evolves and adapts itself to
       confront the complex issues referred to in the seminar.

Learning in a Knowledge Society
John Cassels

I shall discuss four issues. The work and nature of the National Commission on Education; the nature of a knowledge society and its implications for education; some particular questions about post-school education; and where we ought to be in 20-35 years time, if we have successfully reformed our education.

The Commission was a private, independently funded venture. We were encouraged at the outset by the very fine work done by a number of private ventures in the educational field, such as the Carnegie Institute for the Advancement of Teaching.

There were 16 Commissioners, roughly half of whom might be described as educationalists; others came from industry, and other walks of life. From the start it was determinedly research-based and non-political.

Terms of Reference

We were asked to cover all phases of education from the cradle to the grave, and to include issues of training.

We covered the whole of the United Kingdom: this was

important in the light of unwillingness in different parts of the country to notice what goes on elsewhere.

We were asked to look 25 years ahead, and we wanted from the outset to reach a wide public, which is why we published a paperback in plain, readable English (*Learning to Succeed* (Report of the National Commission on Education), Heinemann, 1993). An important factor concerns not the detail of what we say but the underlying principles.

The Knowledge Society

The fundamental contrast is between the industrial revolution on the one hand, and the knowledge revolution which is now proceeding apace - and the very different implications of those two revolutions for education and training.

The industrial revolution, which reached its high point in this country between 1780 and 1850, depended on neither a high level of education nor a high level of training. That being so, it did not seem economically important to the politically conscious people and legislators to improve the level of education. Efforts to improve education depended on other reasons.

To reinforce that point: in 1913 Britain's main exports,

especially throughout the Empire, were cotton and cotton goods. We exported 100 million tons of coal in 1913. Our other great export was iron and steel, the production of which involved only moderate levels of science and "advanced" science and technology. We can now see that by 1913 these industries were entering a steep decline. Earlier on, in 1902, the Board of Education in England chose as its model for secondary education the public school. It was not thought the right thing that British children should learn expedient studies; they should learn studies which would improve their morals and would tend to virtue. Scotland was the first part of the country which had universal secondary education for all, for a few weeks in 1939, and it pre-dated the Butler Act of 1944 - the great Education Reform Act in England. The 1944 Act provided for three kinds of school in England and Wales: grammar school (the established model from the past); technical school (an innovation and one clearly connected with work and with industry); and secondary modern school for other children. In practice the grammar schools flourished; the technical schools hardly made any progress at all - about 2% of pupils at the high level were going to technical schools in England and Wales. But if the technical schools never took off, the secondary modern schools lacked clear vision and standards. This was because it was still thought that there wasn't much connection between education and work.

In the last three decades all has changed. First there has been the "knowledge revolution". Quoting from Peter Drucker's *Post-Capitalist Society*, we can say that in a knowledge society:

> The basic economic resource - 'the means of production' to use the economist's term - is no longer capital, nor natural resources (the economist's 'land'), nor 'labour'. *It is and will be knowledge.*

Dr. Hermann Schmidt, the Director of the Institute of Vocational Education in Berlin, has brilliantly characterised the differences between the traditional form of a company, or organisation, (which he calls 'Before Japan' companies, or 'BJ' for short), and modern companies that have learned from Japanese success (known as 'After Japan' companies). In a traditional organisation you are not asking for a great deal by way of initiative from the people at the bottom. You are asking primarily for an ability to carry out instructions. The great drawback of that kind of organisation is that it is not possible to concentrate all the wisdom of a company into a few people at the top. In a modern company hierarchy doesn't matter greatly, nor does it need to have several layers: instead there are groups of people each of whom are expected to share in the responsibility for doing things, for making things, for solving problems and so on. In such modern organisations there is a need for people who have high levels of education, high levels of

11

training and high levels of ability.

The Institute for Employment Research at Warwick University which has studied trends in employment for some 15 years, finds that in the next decade there will be big increases in the employment of managers, administrators and professional occupations. Conversely blue-collar jobs are going to decrease fairly fast.

A similar occupational breakdown for 1970 - a little over 20 years ago - shows that the blue-collar workers then outnumbered others by some 5 million in Great Britain. In the year 2000 blue-collar workers will themselves be outnumbered by over 3 million. That again emphasises the huge advantage to those who have had a good education and training because they can have access to knowledge jobs.

An earnings table covering the decade 1979-89 (taken from *Social Trends*) indicates the real income, after housing costs, of the bottom 20%, middle 20% and top 20% of the population. There was no change at all in the real income of those at the bottom; there is a significant increase for those in the middle; and the top 20% did well.

12

<u>Median net real income after housing costs by</u>
<u>quintile group 1979 and 1988-89, United Kingdom</u>

£ per week at 1992 prices

Year	Quintile group of individuals		
	Bottom fifth	Middle fifth	Top fifth
1979	81	143	253
1988-89	81	176	355

(Source: *Social Trends* 23, 1993 Edition, Table 5.18)

These income variations are not simply the result of taxation changes.

Some of the effects of the knowledge society can be altered one way or another by social policy, but it should be clearly recognised that social cohesion tends to diminish in the knowledge society.

15% of 21 year olds have the greatest difficulty in being able to read and write well enough to be able to use it, or for it to be functional either at work or in leisure; and that proportion is higher still with numbers - something like 20%. The National Commission on Education summarised its view of the 1993 position in Britain as follows:

> A minority of academically able young people receive a good, if narrow, education and, for them, provision is well suited and efficiently run. For a majority of young people, education is of more variable benefit. The talents of many are not valued enough and not developed enough; and, once they start work, the same is true in terms of training. In addition, an uncomfortably large minority of young people leaving school have trouble with literacy and numeracy...

Questions

Five questions arise. The first concerns the cost of educating the whole population to a high level: how can it be paid for? The first inevitable step is that students themselves will have to contribute to the cost of education. There will be incidental benefits, because students who pay tend to value their education more than those who do not.

To tackle the problems of illiteracy and innumeracy, in contexts where the home is not the ideal learning place, we shall need to make huge investment in high quality nursery education.

Secondly, there is increasing and welcome acceptance throughout Britain, and not only in Scotland, that greater emphasis must be placed on vocational education. In Scotland there are the Scottish vocational qualifications and in England and Wales the National Council for Vocational Qualifications is pressing on down the same road. Such a conversion represents a huge change in the values overtly embodied in our higher education system but vocational education is now accepted, by right-thinking people, as inevitably and desirably part of the higher education system.

Thirdly, in a much expanded post-school situation, much greater attention than in the past must be given to high quality teaching, even if the former emphasis on university research is diminished.

Fourthly, in the kind of world we have moved into, continuing learning is already with us on rather a large scale: over 12 million people in Britain each year have some continuing education. The engine for it is industry because industry needs people to learn new things in order to be up to date. It would be a disastrous mistake if, in developing the higher education system for the future, we stuck to the idea, either implicitly or explicitly, that the important thing was the first degree and that we should continue to concentrate on people of 18 and 19 coming into university, spending three years, getting a degree and going away. We do not want to extend that model in general. Knowledge becomes out of date very quickly. What we do want is to have a situation where people understand the need to come back often, and are enabled to do so.

Finally, I wanted to make an obeisance of some kind towards technology. Whatever technology becomes available for enabling people to learn, the teacher remains a teacher (not a mere 'facilitator') because he or she should know how people learn and what they need.

Conclusion

The future? 20 years from now virtually every child who emerges from school must have good standards of literacy and numeracy. Then, all young people must continue their education at least to 18 or 19, and most should acquire something of a more up to date equivalent of 'A' levels. Perhaps 60% of our people will go into graduate study at once and there should be a continuing coming back into education throughout life.

The question of social cohesion needs final emphasis. There are very serious problems raised by the knowledge society and by the difference between those with knowledge and without

16

knowledge, and those in intensive/high knowledge jobs and those with very little. I leave you with the Commission's Vision:

1. In all countries *knowledge* and *applied intelligence* have become central to economic success and personal and social well-being.
2. In the United Kingdom much higher achievement in education and training is needed to match world standards.
3. Everyone must want to learn and have ample opportunity and encouragement to do so.
4. All children must achieve a good grasp of literacy and basic skills early on as the foundation for learning throughout life.
5. The full range of people's abilities must be recognised and their development rewarded.
6. High-quality learning depends above all on the knowledge, skill, effort and example of teachers and trainers.
7. It is the role of education *both* to interpret and pass on the values of society *and* to stimulate people to think for themselves and to change the world around them.

Discussion

In discussion it was pointed out that the economic impact of education was always much better understood in Scotland than in England; indeed it was the means by which Scots achieved personal,

17

social, economic mobility, and it certainly contributed to significant emigration of qualified Scots around the world.

There has also been much better understanding in Scotland of the vocational relevance of education. Since education was practical, a balance between knowing about and knowing how to was effortlessly achieved within the framework of higher education, and there was no artificial distinction between 'knowledge' and 'skills'. In Scotland the Secretary of State, it might be noted, is responsible for both education and training.

The Schmidt model of company organisation/management, 'before' and 'after Japan', also described the concept of custodianship of quality, the way in which the quality control process has changed; and the way in which the custodianship of standards has passed from one's superior, to oneself.

On the question of who is going to pay, it is notable that the Higher Education Funding Councils in Britain do not reward outputs at all; by providing funds they simply enable institutions to take in inputs. The individual student's contribution to the higher educational process seems to consist of the cash outlay on his/her maintenance during the higher educational period; the opportunity cost of the time which they devote at that commonly post-school period; and least significantly, the marginal contribution to the actual costs of the process of learning and being taught. In such a scenario the costs of being economically advantaged tend not to be borne by the beneficiary of the economic advantage. The same is true of training; the employer who provides training equips his employee with a higher earning capability and greater mobility. So the balance of cost and benefit seems to be unequally distributed in the training as well as in higher education.

The balance between the rewards for teaching and the rewards for research is an important issue at present for the British academic community. In the UK when the university population expanded very dramatically in the 1960s, the central technical colleges were allowed to become much more like older universities than is the hope of the present expansion. The hope now is to retain a greater diversity of mission than was achieved thirty years ago. Excellence is attainable in a variety of forms.

Three types of continuing education - updating, remedial and widening - can be related to either vocational requirements or to recreational leisure requirements.

In Britain there is still a struggle to break away from a Victorian model in which the convenience of the few teachers is maximised over those of large numbers of students. As one moves further away from the post-school leaver as the natural university entrant, towards continuing education, student immobility and inflexibility become greater problems because of the other demands on their time and physical location.

The issue of social cohesion is very important. If education is regarded as a means of economic wealth creation, it is vital to ensure that those whom you have educated stay and deploy their skills to create wealth in the very community from which they have derived their own personal advantage. That, of course, was what Scotland was unable fully to do during the 18th and 19th centuries.

How far should the economic value or benefit figure in one's assessment of education? Should those concerned with education be less concerned to follow actual trends than to formulate values and ideals that ought to be upheld in the future? The notion of 'utility' can be misunderstood. In the Scottish Enlightenment, it was understood broadly and was central to the emphasis on education for the improvement of society. Rooted in concern for practical benefits, education sought to keep together all the perspectives we now separate into arts and sciences. Almost all educational endeavours can be properly linked to vocational concerns. When discussing the 'utility' of various studies or disciplines it is important to establish appropriate timescales for judging the utility. In some cases it is easily judged because it is easily quantified, and over a short timescale: in other cases their true value only emerges over a longer period.

One reason for the relative success of vocational education on the Continent, in contrast to England, lies in the broader conception of education on the Continent. For example, the entry to technical institutes requires prior passes in philosophy. Technological awareness must be part of the general education of everyone, and reference to vocational study must not omit or disguise this need.

In Britain there are very very large numbers of children between 12 and 15 who do not see the relevance of what they were being taught to their own lives. It was thought that in certain respects the judges of what is useful and desirable must be the pupils themselves, because their motivation and application depend on their ability to link their studies to their own lives.

Breadth and Balance in Post-Compulsory Education
John Howie

In many countries, the legal compulsion to attend a school ends at age 16, so in talking of post-compulsory education I want especially to refer to the phase from 16 to 18. I shall call it 'Upper Secondary Education'.

It is almost universal in education systems that the curriculum is totally specified up to the age of 14 or so, and that choice is severely limited up to age 16. And this is surely as it should be: children are in no position to make rational choices, and it is our duty to keep as many avenues open to them as we possibly can. Equally, all systems I have heard about do allow a degree of choice after the end of compulsory education, and the crucial question for planners of an education system is over how much choice should be permitted.

In one sense, to argue in favour of breadth and balance is like stating a preference for virtue over vice. But in fact it is not as simple as that, for different educational systems have vastly different approaches. At one extreme is the English 'A' Level system, with its intense concentration on three, or even two subjects. At the other extreme one finds the various continental European systems. For example, consider the weekly timetable for the French Baccalauréat 'C', the one subtitled 'Mathematics and Physics'. (In England the corresponding student might well be spending two thirds of his time on mathematics and a third on physics.)

Subject	Hours per week
French	3
Philosophy	3
Social Studies	4
Mathematics	9
Physics/Chemistry	5
Biology	2
Foreign Language 1	2
Foreign Language 2	2
Industrial Arts/Home Economics	3
Art	2
Physical Education	2
Economics	2
TOTAL	39

An overall award is given, with the subjects weighted roughly in proportion to the time spent on them.

Now the fact that two closely similar societies separated by a narrow sea channel adopt such different strategies suggests that the issue is not as clear-cut as one might at first suppose. In favour of the English approach one might advance a number of arguments.

1. It achieves high standards in the chosen subjects, and prepares the students well for the unusually short university courses that are the norm in England.

2. Because students are in classes that they have chosen, their motivation is high and the class atmosphere is good.

3. (closely related to the last two points). Teachers gain a great deal of satisfaction from the teaching at advanced levels of well-motivated students.

4. The level to which subjects are taken, and the two year time scale involved, encourages the development of sound study skills.

On the debit side one might record:

1. The implication that science specialists need not study even their own language means that the ability of scientifically trained students even to write a coherent technical report is not what it might be.

2. Students who specialise in humanities at this early stage remain ignorant of science to an extent that is quite frightening.

3.   (a distinct but related point). Many students leave school
        with a debilitating degree of mathematical and statistical
        ignorance.

4.   Premature specialisation can lead to a poor choice of further
        study and/or career. In my own department, some students
        from England, having been entered on a mathematics track
        from an early age, turn out to be neither very good at it nor
        very fond of it.

In summary, there can be little doubt that the English
approach contributes to what Charles Snow called 'The Two
Cultures' divide in British society, and in particular to a widespread
lack of numeracy.

In favour of the French approach one might claim that:

1.   It sets out to create well-informed citizens, and it must
        succeed at least some of the time. Many of the streets in the
        Sorbonne area of Paris are named after mathematicians, and
        (perhaps naively) I suppose that most educated French
        people know at least a little about (say) Legendre, and his
        contribution to learning. By contrast, I could find a high
        degree of ignorance among allegedly educated people in
        Britain concerning (say) James Clerk Maxwell, a vastly more
        important figure than Legendre in the history of ideas.

2. It has the effect of postponing career choice to an age when truly adult decisions can be made.

3. While the standards attained in individual subjects cannot be as high as in the English system, a high achievement ethos can develop within the group of students studying a particular version of the <u>Bac</u>, as they move from subject to subject within the curriculum.

4. The group approach makes it very much easier to exhibit cross-fertilisation between subjects.

On the debit side one might list the following points:

1. The prospect of having to do disliked subjects might discourage staying on.

2. The minor subjects receive a shallow treatment.

3. Students may be poorly motivated, even hostile, in some of their classes.

4. Mental blocks are excessively penalised.

Now there are some genuine problems here. The evidence from France and other countries, however, suggests that staying on rates are at least as high as they are in England, and so the fear in (1) is probably not reflected in what would actually happen in this country. As for (2), there is no doubt that minor subjects receive shallow treatment. Some, however, quote Alexander Pope as their authority in support of the extraordinary claim that the information gained is <u>worse</u> than useless:

A little learning is a dangerous thing,

Drink deep, or taste not the Pierian spring.

- tacitly assuming, no doubt, that Pope has the kind of infallibility that attaches to his name. It seems to me more accurate, if less poetic, to believe that a little learning is better than none at all. So, allowing that the knowledge gained in minor subjects within the <u>Bac</u> does not amount to much, I would still claim that the young person in France is better prepared for life than his or her English counterpart.

The third point is a genuine one, and there is an associated danger, that standards in compulsory subjects creep downwards. When a pass in Latin was a prerequisite for the ordinary M.A. degree in Scottish universities, the status accorded to the subject had no beneficial effect either on the syllabus or the standards. It is important within a group system to allow compensation, so that in any compulsory subject a performance that is below pass standard but not too disastrously weak can be compensated for by good performance elsewhere - and this is in effect what happens with a Baccalaureate system.

Mental blocks do exist, though, like tone deafness in music, they are probably not as common as is claimed. And of course, the most common academic mental block is in mathematics. The French acknowledge the problem. In considering the basis on which students make their choices from within the many lettered variants of the Bac, a document[2] from the French Ministry of Education makes the worrying point that

> ...on trouve les élèves regroupés non pas en fonction de leurs goûts pour les sciences experimentales (D), l'économie (B), les lettres (A), les techniques de gestion (G), mais en fonction de leur inaptitude croissante à suivre en mathematiques!
>
> Ce système, rigide, aboutit à une perversion de l'orientation et ne permet de changement d'orientation que dans le sens descendant d'une hiérarchie construite sur un critère unique.

The French are seeking solutions within their own structures, and they regard it as inconceivable that they might go over to an à la carte system like the English (or for that matter the Scots). What I have seen of their mathematics syllabuses suggests that a more imaginative and user-friendly approach there would go some way towards solving the problem.

The English system has its supporters, crucially within the

ranks of Her Majesty's Government, but also within the independent schools. These facts are probably not unconnected: the independent schools seem to be almost the only source from which the English Department for Education seems prepared to take advice. I can understand the stance of the independent schools more easily than I can that of the Government. The formal examinable curriculum is only part of the story, and especially in boarding schools, where the 'hidden curriculum' is, for good or ill, extremely pervasive. Young people absorb an ethos, and learn perhaps more from each other than from their teachers. Where the Government makes its mistake is in supposing that the same process of osmosis can happen automatically in the sixth form of a city comprehensive school. It can happen, but the curriculum must be designed so as to encourage it to happen.

The independent schools provide one focus of support for the Government's policy. It is hard to find another. The University Vice-Chancellors, the Royal Society[5], Save British Science, the National Commission on Education[6], Industry - almost every organ of what used to be called The Establishment has publicly denounced the system. Even the Higginson Report[3] commissioned by the government itself, could find little to say in favour of the status quo. Both the Royal Society and Save British Science came out in favour of the International Baccalaureate.

To some extent Scotland ploughs an independent furrow in educational matters. Its right to do so in an otherwise unitary and highly centralised state is widely believed to go back to the Act of Union of 1707, when Scotland agreed to become part of a United Kingdom. There are two crucial aspects in which the Scottish system differs from the English. First, university degree courses are typically four years in duration as opposed to three. Secondly, the academically able young people who in England would be taking three 'A' levels at age 18, in Scotland are taking five Highers at age 17.

For this reason, Scots have always prided themselves on the breadth of their education. Certainly five subjects is to be preferred to three, but when the Howie Committee carried out an examination of what actually happens it found a picture less rosy than any of us had expected. Of boys taking five Highers at age 17, only 25% included a language other than English. There were other glaring defects, mainly arising from over-examining within the school system as a whole and from a resulting pattern of jerky progress: instead of a smooth upward incline between 12 and 18 our young people were progressing by means of a mixture of cliff faces and plateaux. On the issues of breadth and balance, we were forced to conclude that only in comparison with the English system was the Scottish system performing well.

Indeed, after a great deal of hesitation, we convinced ourselves that only a group system along the lines of the French or International Baccalaureate could deliver the kind of balance we wanted to see. I am very disappointed indeed that the Secretary of State for Scotland and his colleagues have not been similarly convinced. In the recently published document *Higher Still*[4] the Government appears to accept our diagnosis of the ills of the present system and our list of desirable characteristics for a reformed system, but has not accepted this crucial aspect of our proposed remedy. There is some exhortation on the theme of breadth or balance, but I am unconvinced that exhortation is enough.

In the Howie Report[1] we had a good deal to say about values. Under the general heading Aims and Characteristics and the subheading Attitudes, Values and Motives we wrote:

> Assistance to young people in formulating values and principles to guide their behaviour; moral and religious development, desirable propensities including concern and compassion for others; intellectual honesty; tolerance and fairness; respect for and a willingness to employ rational approaches to issues and problems; resourcefulness and enterprise; open-mindedness; awareness of major social issues; an appetite for learning; qualities of

curiosity and interest; the capacity to enjoy the arts, literature and the media; and the mix of opportunity and responsibility implied in their own growing confidence and understanding.

The problem is to run an education system in which even the teachers, never mind the pupils, come close to the paragon status implied by the paragraph.

The issue now is how to devise an upper secondary system that will give maximum encouragement to young people, at this crucial stage between adolescence and full adulthood, to develop in the ways we want to see. A slot in the timetable labelled 'values' is not the whole answer, though I suppose that it might make a contribution. I am no supporter of separate Catholic education, but I do accept the point made by various church leaders that lessons in RE are only part of the point, that it is the total Catholic ethos in a school that matters most of all. It is similarly so with the less doctrinal approach to values we espoused in the Howie Report: the whole ethos of the school must encourage and enhance these qualities.

I submit that within a group system it may be somewhat easier to ensure that this happens, for one can predict the entire curriculum of a student. In an à la carte system it is all too easy for these crucial matters to fall into the gap between subjects.

REFERENCES

1.   *Upper Secondary Education in Scotland*, (The Howie Report), HMSO, March 1992.
2.   *Propositions de Conseil National des programmes sur l'Evolution du Lycée, Premier Rapport*, Ministère de l'Education Nationale, de la Jeunesse, et des Sports, Novembre 1990.
3.   *Advancing A Levels* (The Higginson Report), HMSO, April 1988.
4.   *Higher Still: Opportunity for All*, The Scottish Office, March 1994.
5.   *Beyond GCSE*, The Royal Society, May 1991.
6.   *Learning to Succeed* (Report of the National Commission on Education), Heinemann, 1993.

Discussion

It was pointed out that the Howie Committee consciously decided not to examine the Japanese system in depth, not only because of major differences in the system and society, but also because it did not wish to change the length of the school week in Scotland, or the balance of work between schoolwork or homework. [The length of the week in school in Scotland is 25/27 hours and in France 39 hours].

The Howie report argued that one of the things wrong in the Scottish system is "the two-term dash": students between 16 and 17 have to cover an enormous amount of material, and their courses are far too examination directed. With a longer time horizon and with various assessments during the course contributing to the final grade, it was felt that pupils would achieve a greater depth and breadth.

The Howie report suggested a Baccalaureate up to age 18 for up to 40% of the population and for the remaining 60% suggested a certificate (a two year affair ending at age 17) on the whole more vocationally-based. In hindsight the Committee accepts that it presented its recommendation as involving more of a divide than it intended. The French have various kinds of Baccalauréat, but nobody pretends that there is no pecking order within the Bacs in France. There is a well defined hierarchy ranging from the mathematics and physics one at the top to the Bac Professionnel (the vocational one) at the bottom. But the pupil can say he has passed the Bac and there is a status attaching to that.

34

The Committee also now believes that it showed a lack of vision in believing that the certificate should end at 17, whereas the system was already changing rapidly, with 70% of present day pupils volunteering to stay on after 16. Against such changes the Committee could have made its recommendation look much more like the Baccalauréat and avoided this impression of divisiveness. The Committee found no straightforward correlation between specialisation and motivation. Some students find early specialisation very attractive, but often for not very good reasons. It could be argued that instead of having three subjects in which one tries to go into depth (as in the 'A' level system), in the French system there is really one subject which is treated in depth: for example, 9 hours per week of mathematics indicates that there is at least one area in which they are going to go into depth.

The question was raised of how to prepare teachers, from the primary stages of education upwards, for the strenuous tasks of making value systems explicit, and developing awareness in their pupils of values. It was agreed that Britain compared adversely with some other countries in preparing young people for general citizenship. We should not be frightened to tackle rather sensitive current issues - e.g. genetic engineering.

In North America, the attempt to study medical ethics as a

separate ethics course, independently of medical science, failed. Ethics questions must be raised in science lessons but also in the social sciences, especially in pluralistic societies. To do this appropriately and effectively will probably require changes in teacher training as well as in particular disciplinary curricula. Young people working for companies that are thinking in European terms, will have to be increasingly flexible, to be willing to work in other European countries, and have to be competent in foreign languages.

A major difference between the cultures and attitudes of Britain, on the one hand, and East Asian communities, on the other, concerns the distinction between ability and effort. In East Asian traditions effort is more important than ability, and learning is about effort.

Many now agree with the separation of church and state in schools, but one can distinguish between religious education, and worship. Religion has been a major part of human history, civilisation and experience, and one way to avoid religious illiteracy is to teach about religion in schools: about Christianity, Judaism, Islam, Hinduism, Buddhism. If we are aiming for tolerance, understanding and respect for others, it is vital to gain knowledge of the grounding values of different cultures and traditions.

The Fading Away of an Educated Public
Victoria Camps

Connecting education and values brings into the open one of the great contradictions of our age. We realize that education ought in future to have a role in solving the crisis that civilization faces. But this education, on which we would like to rely, is in fact being adapted increasingly to the demands of a system that is taking us into a dead-end: an economic system that is producing serious pockets of poverty and unemployment; technology for which we are inadequately prepared; and a political organization that ducks all serious problems. As Vaclav Havel recently wrote, the West seems to have lost the capacity for self-sacrifice - a capacity that can only be promoted through education. But educational systems either do not want to have anything to do with the problem, or do not know where to begin. On the one hand, we preach interminably about the values that education should transmit, while at the same time we accept that the educational system should be guided by utilitarian and pragmatic aims and emptied of everything that does not seem economically profitable. Hence arises the contradiction about which I propose to speak today.

It is best for me to begin with a simple definition of education, which I trust will be acceptable. To educate is, in one way or another, 'to teach how to live'. Anything that involves giving a certain meaning to life, guiding or directing it, is what, according to its etymology, 'education' means. If the aim of education is to help the child or young person connect herself in the widest sense with life, then the values of education should be mainly ethical or moral ones; for these are the values that have, since time began, endeavoured to produce tolerance, social cohesion and, sometimes, individual happiness. The places where education goes on are primarily the family and school, later perhaps university. They function in different ways. At school the child enters a world of less personal relationships and more structured teaching, she feels she is not alone but one among many, and comes into contact with differences that do not exist in the nuclear family. She faces the need, not only to learn the minimum rules of mutual respect, but to learn what are considered the basic facts of knowledge and culture. Other sources of knowledge and information supplement the efforts of family and school, contributing, for better or for worse, to the child's vision of the world and her way of relating to it. The most important of these sources, as far as children are concerned, is beyond doubt television.

To a considerable extent the idea that education ought to accept any moral values and transmit them has scarcely been accepted by those responsible for education in recent decades.

Fundamentally, I am referring to teachers at all levels and the educational profession in general, but the statement can easily be generalized to include fathers and mothers as well. A set of presuppositions has been the cause of such an education uncertain of its function or its aims. I will summarize them briefly. Firstly, the secularization of education has tended to limit it to mere 'instruction of the public' - a trap of positivism, which insists on regarding schooling as something neutral with regard to ideologies, religions, and doctrines: schools, if they are open to all and free, should restrict themselves to teaching their pupils only what is indispensable to be members of the society in which they are going to live. Secondly, the conflict between authoritarianism and libertarianism, which was especially sharp in my country, ended in the victory of libertarianism. Prohibitions have gone long ago and, with them, have disappeared the rules as well. To educate, in the opinion of libertarians, must not mean repressing or traumatizing the pupil - as if one could get through life without any traumas! The only concession allowed to the educator is to explain some subjects; and, even so, this education - which by definition is tough - must appear 'friendly' and, if possible, amusing. The main thing is that the student should not suffer and should not even realise that he is learning how to work. Besides, if the object of education is to train people to be autonomous in a pluralist and tolerant society, how could such a notion be reconciled with repression and norms?

Thirdly, there was the idea promoted by left-wing doctrines that the economic or social system was to blame for everything. It was the structures and not the people that should be changed so that everything should be better. What was ultimately responsible for unhappiness and injustice is an impersonal abstraction spelt with a capital letter: the State, Religion, Politics, the Market. Finally, scepticism penetrated to our bones, making us suspicious of values that were supposed to be universal. Values are inevitably 'biased', 'partisan', and 'subjective', the expression of someone or other's desire for power. Their only effect is to oppress, and, in any event, they hide instead of revealing the reality of social problems and the meaning of human liberation. Further, the attempt to transmit subjective or biased values is perceived as real cruelty. One should talk to children about what is true and objective and, if that does not exist, it is better not to teach them anything. It is unnecessary to say that behind this cloud of simplifications and absurdities lurk the worst aspects of Marx, Nietzsche, and Freud.

Spain has perhaps displayed the results of such presuppositions more crudely than anywhere else. It was predictable that this might happen if one considers that the transition to democracy involved the end of an exclusively religious educational system, in which specialised instruction, for religious reasons, was severely subordinated to emphasis on complete character formation. Such character training pushed all vocational training into a very inferior position. The establishment of democracy involved the simultaneous extension of education to all. Such equality of opportunity has, however, produced some inevitable consequences: the system deteriorates when it ceases to be élitist.

After only a few years, however, this abdication from the task of education on the part of families and schools has begun to be corrected, doubtless because its errors have become obvious. It has been realized that even instruction is difficult when all moral values are lacking; since, in the end, to learn anything one must perform some sacrifice, be humble, tolerant and co-operative, and submit to some minimal rules, even though these be repressive. Further, we have also realized that there is no reason for so much scepticism: it is not difficult to arrive at some minimal ethical rules, which have emerged from our traditions and taken shape in the form of the universally accepted Declaration of Human Rights. At the same time, we realize that the behaviour of men and women in our world is not so much guided by respect for these rights as by fidelity to other values and principles that have little to do with ethics, and much to do with the economic and political system: success, money, personal glory, competitiveness without scruple.

Such considerations, perhaps, have encouraged those responsible for the Spanish education system to proclaim the importance of education in moral values. The preamble to our

General Law for the Organization of the Educational System (LOGSE) contains phrases like "the complete character development" of the person, the "formation of the individual identity", the need to teach how to "evaluate" reality as well as to acquire knowledge about it. It refers to such requirements of education as freedom, fellow-feeling, tolerance, democratic community, mutual respect, and the struggle against discrimination and inequality. The new law clearly declares in favour of a form of education that, as well as passing on knowledge, should help one criticize and evaluate it.

As the implementation of this law progresses, it is taking on a clearly utilitarian character. The Spanish educational system, like others, has for some time been watching impotently while the humanities disappeared before the advance of scientific and technical subjects. Despite insistence that the 'quality' of education depended fundamentally on its transmission of moral values, it is hard to reconcile such good intentions with the ways in which the content of education is actually regulated. The necessary modernization of education is taken to mean progress according to criteria of an effective vocational training, rather than of character training designed to teach one how to live. The time devoted to basic subjects has been reduced: literature, art, philosophy, history; not to mention Latin and Greek, which by now nobody remembers. The old division of the sixth-form course between humanities and sciences has been diversified by adding one course called 'technological' and another called 'artistic'. To sum up, practical studies are becoming as relevant as theoretical ones. To get into university, it is as important to acquire techniques as to study the classics.

I wonder - and we are all wondering - how to overcome the double difficulty that an education in ethical values involves today. I say a double difficulty because on the one hand we have to get over the prejudices that I mentioned earlier and accept that schools and universities have to educate - with all the implications this has. On the other hand, if to educate means creating autonomous people, capable of thinking for themselves, then it also means training critical minds. How can this be done if we can count less and less on the excellent mental equipment provided by the humanities for such training? What can be done if education is proving ever more incapable of arousing enthusiasm to read or of developing appreciation of writing and language? What will happen if the need to read goes on fading from the curriculum? If the classics are never read, if our traditions and history are unknown, and if the past is never considered, it will be pretty difficult to rediscover those values that ought to help us criticize the reality around us.

I realize that the situation I describe is not unique to my country. From what I read and hear, the decline of the humanities is just as general as the feeling that something essential is missing in our educational system, as it adapts itself to a society in which economics and technology reign supreme. A group of French teachers lamented recently in *Le Monde* (2 April 1993) that Efficiency, Productivity, Profitability are the values that have pushed aside the republican motto: Liberty, Equality, Fraternity. Do we want a society that cannot avoid replacing those enlightened values by economic ones? It seems that we have all thrown in the towel in the face of an omnipotent economic system that is to all intents and purposes indispensable. If schools do not "dare to educate", which means "awakening the moral consciousness" of the pupil at the same time as she is taught, it will be hard for us to succeed in improving a society in which violence and divisiveness are advancing each and every day.

The dilemma in which we find ourselves is not easy to solve. To realize that we face problems is, however, the first step towards finding solutions. I spoke at the beginning of the fantasies which still obsess us and do not allow us to appreciate education as we should. If to educate correctly means to teach individuals how to be independent, it is essential to abandon our scepticism and put order into our system of ideas. If anybody is to reach a state of autonomy, she must be taught things: she must be shown how to love some kind of world, personal and social relationships, and to despise what we believe is valueless. It is necessary to form habits and customs, and taste so as to appreciate what we consider good and reject what we consider bad; all of which means the ability to distinguish one thing from another and the desire to transmit this ability. To teach anyone to think for herself one must start with some content, some concepts, some ideas, about which one can then think. Convictions and beliefs have to exist before you can criticize them. Education cannot be initially or exclusively self-critical. It must start by teaching a culture and traditions that are not totally contemptible. Otherwise one arrives in the contradictory position of trying to train someone in how to criticize without first having taught anything that can be criticized. Many young people of today, disillusioned, mixed-up, and apathetic, have experienced only such pseudo-education, along with the formulation of expectations that had no relation to reality.

Hence, to be able to steer in the right direction again, specific knowledge is a help and not a hindrance. Education must include information about the world we have inherited and wish to preserve, and at the same time it should train people to be critical of this world; to do which, Plato, St. Augustine, Shakespeare or Cervantes will be more useful than a chemical experiment or a telecommunications system. In the last analysis technological applications produce problems that are not just technical. They are philosophical.

All the same, it is not the cultivated man but the

technologist who is the characteristic figure of our age. And this figure is producing a change in our values since the criterion by which a technical product is judged is how well it functions: a technical product has to function, since that was all it was made for. A car must run without breaking down, a washing machine must leave clothes clean; a telephone should transmit voices well. The value of a technologist's work is justified by its perfect adjustment to the purpose of making a product. Such activity was called poiesis by Aristotle, to distinguish it from praxis, human activity proper to a human being that was justified by ethical criteria or values. In other words, technology imposes as the ultimate value - efficiency. This same value is the one by which that other figure of our age, the manager, operates. What is important is results, the efficacy of what is done.

This priority of efficiency over every other consideration makes the technologist incapable of facing 'the totality of the technical action', that is the sum of factors that interact in it, which may unleash dysfunctions or negative externalities, unexpected consequences and, above all, inconvenient results for society from the point of view of its other values. An effective clothes-drier may nevertheless produce severe pollution; a successful experiment in genetic engineering, such as the cloning of embryos, may be idiotic from a social point; television, a mass medium that could be very useful for education, may be - and usually is - perverse as an

46

educational tool. But these social goals or functions do not worry the technologist because his vision is limited to the specific product. Wider criticism and evaluation of his work from an equally 'functional' but more global perspective is outside his concerns.

The activities and attitudes of the technologist have finally contaminated those of all specialists. The division and extension of knowledge has so fragmented every field of study that we know less and less about things in general and more and more about tiny and narrow detail. Hence springs the corporativism that is all too obvious in the academic world. Everyone, including the humanists, is interested only in what concerns her work, her publication, or her experiment. Common interest is disappearing from everybody's field of vision. It is not surprising that politicians are going in the same direction and that they end up finding that organizing their own affairs - the party - is of more interest than society's problems and conflicts.

However, to return to technical education, I said earlier that to educate must necessarily mean to teach 'something', to transfer some content. The technical mentality has led us to obliterate all content. We demand technical perfection of the television, of our kitchen equipment, of computers, and of motorways; and we consider hardly or not at all the sense or purpose of all these facilities, apart from the immediate comfort provided. The excellence of the

47

<u>hardware</u> worries us more than that of the <u>software</u>. Sometimes we waste or under-use numerous technical inventions; and sometimes they turn against us, causing us unexpected trouble and labour. The danger of technology, in one of Heidegger's most epigrammatic phrases, is that "it hides from man the truth about his own nature, about himself, and about God".

We glimpse this truth when we start questioning ourselves about 'the quality of our lives'; or when we ask ourselves whether technical advance has any connexion with moral advance. Hans Jonas has reformulated Kant's categorical imperative as follows: "Act in such a way that the consequences of your actions may be compatible with the continuance of human life in a genuine sense." This imperative should form the criterion by which all that we do must be judged. Does technology humanize or dehumanize? What can we hope for from it? Whose job is it to evaluate it? Do we have any paradigm for humanity?

Our need to make ethics into an 'applied' discipline for medicine, nursing, government administration, business, and journalism says a lot about how fundamental values have sunk into oblivion. The figure of the competent professional - whether he be technologist, manager, or academic - who occupies himself only with what his profession requires of him, so as to excel in it and compete with his colleagues, is not a satisfactory definition of what we would

48

like to consider a 'good person', and it is to produce such a person that education should aim - to find the man who is, to quote the line of Antonio Machado

en todos los sentidos de la palabra, bueno

(in every sense of the word, good)

But such goodness which embraces the whole, and not just some partial aspect, of the person is perhaps something unknowable and, therefore, not practical as an educational aim.

This is, at least, the opinion of the Scottish philosopher, Alasdair MacIntyre, apostle of communitarianism. In his view, we have lost any conception, such as the Greeks or Christian mediaeval philosophers had, of what a person ought to be. Modernity, and the Enlightenment, which was its culmination, put an end to any possibility of an universal ethic. The principles that could form the basis for ethics lack any universally acceptable and rational foundation. Our societies, being a mixture of different cultures, are too plural and dissimilar to come to any agreement on common values. Neither utilitarianism nor human rights - the two ethical models of our epoch - will serve: the first because it is false, and the second because there is no rational justification for human rights.

This diagnosis inevitably affects any educational project. In his article "The Idea of an Educated Public" - a title to which my own title for this paper is indebted - MacIntyre accepts that the two

49

aims of education are impossible because they are incompatible. Education has always proposed: 1) to adapt the young person to a specific social role or function; 2) to teach the young person to think for himself. The two aims would fulfil to perfection the goal outlined at the beginning of this paper as inherent to education: to teach how to live. However, MacIntyre thinks that professional training is nowadays incompatible with the acquisition of a broad culture which would serve as a basis for knowing how to live on one's own account, the sapere aude with which Kant defined the Enlightenment.

The same philosopher explains the reason for the incompatibility by saying that one can think for oneself only if one does not think exclusively for oneself, ignoring everyone else. In other words, what we lack is a community as a nucleus. We do not have a discussion community, sharing its beliefs and attitudes, in which sacred or canonical texts are agreed upon, and where there is no conflict about the criteria that validate and ensure the triumph of any given assertion. This community - which is not Habermas's universal community of dialogue - does not exist in the 20th century. It did exist at other times in history in some places. MacIntyre thinks that 18th century Edinburgh did have this kind of community, thanks to a large extent to the reform of its university by Principal William Carstares. There was a wide group of people who knew what ought to be discussed and how to reach agreement. Today, on the other hand, we neither know what has to be discussed nor the proper way to bring arguments to a conclusion. Discussion about the practical questions which really worry people is outside the field of scientists and intellectuals, who are only interested in being 'erudite' inside their speciality. The educated public have been replaced by a set of specialists. Thinking for oneself has degenerated into something different - thinking according to the rules of one's profession. Not even inter-disciplinary contact is possible because, with the multiplication of academic faculties owing to the specialization of knowledge, the question of the mutual relationship of academic disciplines has been excluded from the terms of each and every one of them. MacIntyre concludes laconically that the professors are the lost hope of modern Western culture.

I share with MacIntyre some of his thesis and admire him for his brilliant diagnosis. But I believe his diagnosis is wrong. It is true that knowledge has become professionalized and that the different branches of learning tend, as they emerge, to shut themselves up in an ivory tower and separate themselves completely from the rest, from which they have in fact sprung. Without any doubt, an educated public is lacking in our time. But I do not think that a community - in the sense of 18th century Scottish community - should be the solution to the incompatibility of the aims of education. I do not believe either that there is really total conflict about fundamental ethical values, as MacIntyre claims there is in this plural multi-cultural era.

The apparent disagreements on fundamental ethical values are no more than the result of the corporativism and specialization of the various branches of science. It is also a result of the presuppositions produced by the demise of the great ideologies: fear of dogmatism, of authoritarianism, and of freedom itself. But it is not true that there are no values we share; it is only that nobody has the job of thinking about them, developing them, explaining what sense they have, or ought to have, for mankind at the end of the 20th century. No-one has the job of doing it because everyone is living in her own minute and exclusive world. The mentality of the technologist and manager renders one incapable of speaking or thinking about matters of general concern, outside the bounds of one's own speciality. As for the intellectuals, who ought to charge at windmills and start discussions about real conflicts, they do not do so because various fears and prejudices hinder them from proclaiming the validity of any moral truth. MacIntyre's thesis, derived partly from analytical philosophy and partly from Marxism, according to which truths are either demonstrated empirically, or justified rationally, or are mere emotional opinions, is at the bottom of all relativism today - for example, of the relativism that rejects human rights as 'Western thought'.

I do not believe, therefore, that we share no basic values.

We share the ideals that have sprung from Christianity and the Enlightenment and the whole tradition of earlier thought going back to the Greeks. This tradition formed an identical morality which cannot vary in different cultures but must accept certain minimum standards, without which neither morals nor ethics would have any stable meaning. If we believe in ethics, we must believe in justice, in liberty, in equality of opportunity, in mutual respect, in tolerance, in co-operation. This agreement exists in theory, though the social practice that exists side by side with such values is another matter. On the other hand, what does not exist is any community concerned with debating, teaching and disentangling the meaning of these values, since there is neither ideological nor intellectual debate and such debate is regarded as lacking interest, prestige and credibility.

Such a community does not exist, not for the reasons given by MacIntyre that there are no agreed principles or shared rules, but because we have diverted our attention towards tasks that divorce us from theoretical and fundamental questions. The diversion of interest towards more functional activities has caused one of the aims of education to push aside the other, but has not made them incompatible. Training to do something useful in life has taken priority and is more important than learning to think for oneself. There is not much time to think so, and learning to do so would be fairly useless. As Benjamin Franklin put it so prophetically, "time is money", so it is better to devote time to something profitable. Branches of learning that cannot show their profitability are useless and should be eliminated or reduced to mere decoration.

Would it be enough to change the curriculum to give more emphasis to the liberal arts and sciences - those that encourage one to think and remind us of our past - to make MacIntyre's two aims of education compatible? To achieve a change of mentality, would it be sufficient to replace a little applied science with pure science? Not unless there is a change of attitude at the same time: a change of mind capable of establishing the conviction that the second aim of education, character training, ought to be as important as the first, vocational training.

In fact, what needs to be done is to recover the "humanist" ideal of education during the Renaissance. The 15th century humanist did not set himself to study the classics just to accumulate knowledge and culture but to understand human nature better. With the studia humanitatis the men of the Renaissance were returning to the Classical tradition but, at the same time, they were inventing a new attitude to knowledge, an attitude that was more practical and more connected to life. They took for granted a truth that was to inspire all modern thought but has begun to be forgotten lately: the centre of knowledge is not God nor nature, but man; and each human being has a dignity that places her above any other living being - a dignity that ought to be preserved at all costs. The humanist ideal wished to escape from the scholastic tradition which had reduced thought to disputations in the scholae, remote from real problems and conflicts.

The scientific and academic corporativism of our times resembles scholasticism more than humanism. The humanist aims of teaching are disappearing in the disputes between different disciplines to acquire greater predominance. Thus dialogue and co-operation between sciences are becoming impossible. To start with, it was religion which prevented the free development of science and, thereby, of human emancipation. Now, however, that same science, transformed into a new god, is putting itself forward as the only reliable and productive form of knowledge and continues to delay the emancipation of mankind by intentionally excluding it from its terms of reference. The 'social sciences', separated from the 'human sciences' - or 'applied sciences' separated from 'pure sciences' - were all born with the aim of being more 'scientific': statistics, field-work, laboratory, and databases bring speculation and theory to an end. We know the positivist ideal well enough: to be scientific means to describe experience, not evaluate it.

Pico della Mirandola, the philosopher who best summarized the humanist ideal, held that a human being "est quamodo omnia" (is in a way everything): she has no predetermined nature but is free to choose the way of life she wishes. That the individual makes herself, is an unfinished, open-ended project, a project of liberty, was to be confirmed centuries later by the existentialist philosophers. But this search for identity and life ideals cannot be a solitary effort; it is a collective task. Hence education with such an aim can only be based on co-operation and joint responsibility between all the branches of knowledge: applied and empirical knowledge as well as pure and speculative knowledge. The former will be more useful to adjust us to the requirements of our existing world. Pure science will serve to remind us of the existence of questions and mysteries which applied science does not even consider.

The opinion of one great philosopher of our century, Ludwig Wittgenstein, was that science has no meaning since it has no answer to the only questions that matter: what should we do and how should we live? The absence of any answers has led the specialists to adopt the morals of the ostrich: il faut cultiver notre jardin and ignore everything else, devoting oneself to what is productive and profitable for its material results and forgetting about wider questions. More than a century ago John Stuart Mill noted the dangers of this dynamic and its educational consequences when he commented that the life of one sex was dedicated to hunting money and the other to breeding money-hunters.

Is it possible to change the direction in which history is

going? Is it possible to reconcile the two aims of education again so that it really teaches how to live? One would have to pursue changes in two fields: reforming the educational system and curricula will, in turn, mean a different, more co-operative and less corporative, attitude to knowledge.

The universities, which are the heart of advanced studies, ought to take the lead in this transformation. Not for nothing will all the teachers charged with the education of the young emerge from the university. To accept this change means realizing that any branch of learning has limitations. No area of study is self-sufficient. Atomization does not help any form of knowledge. The raison d'être of every discipline - physics, biology, medicine, economics, law - lies outside itself because man is not, as Marcuse observed, one dimensional, however much the economic system may try to make it appear as if she were. To be a good doctor, a good lawyer, a good chemist, or a good philologist means more than knowing all the latest theories. Because "professionalism and specialization have broken man to pieces", Ortega y Gasset begged, "let us not become scientific ignoramuses".

If there is no co-operation from inside the teaching system, it is because there is none from outside either; but the educational world, and universities in particular, should give a certain lead in this matter. Spanish universities were the real critical conscience

57

of the country during years of fierce resistance to the established political régime. But criticism died out as the enemy became less clear. The same is happening in Europe: with communism defeated, democracy has been left alone, face to face with itself, without opponents, and obliged to judge itself. In these circumstances, it is simpler to concern oneself with countable and material things than with the post-material or cultural aspects. The Europe of the Community is struggling to acquire economic and political unity; few trouble their heads about the unity of our cultural origins which also involves our spiritual and moral unity.

Universities too have become excessively production-oriented. Nothing is directed towards 'disinterested knowledge'. The universities are investing their resources so as to adapt better to the requirements of a production economy, but do not invest in training that is for the time being 'unproductive', though it be aimed to guide the intellectual and moral faculties of future generations.

We complain that education, teaching, and the universities have lost the prestige they once had. In part this loss is due to the subordination of teaching and education to the criteria - Efficiency, Productivity, Profitability - which dominate everything. To recover its humanistic inspiration education should know how to listen to society without being the slave of all its demands, which are those the market imposes on it. That means, to give one example, daring to redeem the humanities from the relegation and contempt that have befallen them. In order to redeem them, however, one must also dare reform them creatively and imaginatively, finding social functions that they can have apart from preserving a fossilized culture. If humanistic culture is modernized, it will be easier for it to attract the interest of other disciplines and inspire them with a taste for evaluation and criticism. To recollect what human beings have been, what they have said and thought about themselves, recognizing their errors as well as their achievements, is an indispensable foundation for learning to live in the future.

Discussion

It was agreed that common values of some kind are needed to provide a secure foundation for a cohesive society. But we are now living in several societies simultaneously, and above all we are living in a global society. That means that we are competing worldwide, as well as more locally. Our ideas must evolve accordingly. One example of how ideas are changing emerged in the Vienna Conference of June 1993, where it was agreed by many that human rights are not absolute but should be seen through various spectrums.

The humanities enable us to enter imaginatively into cultures and traditions other than our own, but a number of speakers urged that there is no sharp contrast between a scientific education and a humanistic education, since properly taught science is itself a humane study. In the sciences, for example, there is an ethic, a respect for the natural world, for creation (however it came about), and for the achievements of the past - the kind of intellectual effort and ingenuity that went into uncovering the secrets of nature in the past.

Too often a false opposition is established between 'humanitarian' and 'utilitarian'. In the 19th century there was a debate between the Scots on one side, branded as utilitarians, and Newman on the other side. Newman did not have the traditional background of Catholic culture - he hardly knew the work of Thomas Aquinas - and perhaps because of that he asserted that: knowledge is its own end. Had he read Thomas Aquinas's theology he would have known that such a view is treated there as a sin. To seek knowledge for its own end is to commit the sin of <u>curiositas</u>, which is the opposite of what is needed - <u>studiositas</u>. A better definition of education than 'teaching how to live', would be: 'teaching languages'. Physics, for example, is a language in the following two ways. It provides one abstract conceptual framework for looking at the world, in terms of energy, light etc.; the chemist would look at the world from another abstract point of view - that of matter and its composition; and the literary person also looks at the world using the particular framework of individual contingent histories, which nevertheless have a universal value in a paradigmatic kind of way.

The second characteristic of a language possessed by physics is this: learning a language involves talking to someone, not merely talking about the world - so in learning physics, one learns to talk to physicists, and one is entering into the community of physicists, from which one is excluded if one is ignorant of the language. Philosophy is the language which studies these other languages, congregates them together, shows their complementarities, encourages this wholeness of man which Peter Jones has described as essentially Ciceronic. It is thus a mistake to oppose humanities studies with utilitarian studies; on the contrary the utilitarian nature of humanistic studies should be proclaimed and defended. Jobs are given to those who have studied classics because such studies are of a complete culture, including mathematics and theoretical science. An advantage of studying the ancient world was that it was a closed, a defined culture. But an alternative view should also be considered. In the University of Malta, for example, there is a compulsory course for all on the history of Mediterranean civilisation. This begins with a study of the closed classical world, and leads on to a study of the mediaeval world where the cultures of the Muslim and Christian worlds confront each other. Throughout those two periods the Mediterranean world, along with China, was in the avant-garde of world culture. The success of Islam, of the Arabs, in the Middle Ages resulted from connections they established between China and Western Europe, exporting wool from Western Europe and getting silk and spices from the East.

Their resulting prosperity underpinned their ideological constructions. But with the scientific revolution, the Mediterranean becomes a backwater, accelerated by the discovery of America, and the fall of Constantinople. Another factor was the non-acceptance of the implications of the scientific revolution for mistaken, ideological reasons which dominated at the time. These historical examples show how important it is to see science and technology as one of the supreme expressions of humanism. There are scientific, technological languages and there are also mythical, poetical, literary languages. Both are humanist and the complete man needs to have both of them. Whilst few can be a master of both of them at once, all should have an understanding of the different languages well enough for an integrated holistic culture to come about.

Such discussions about the whole man ignore the imperative of the economic man. But the familiar tensions of our day result from the power of democracy to push politicians into trying to meet the economic demands of people for better living standards. Pressures of this kind may increase rather than diminish as competition grows in its intensity, and we face a real problem which is not to be solved within one culture or indeed within one society.

Education for A Fair, Competitive and Interdependent World
John Thomson

I begin with a definition of education: training for life and learning for power, profit and enjoyment. In trying to discern what values education should inculcate, we need to reflect on the relative needs of individuals and of society, together with their own differing values. Questions naturally arise about what needs to be learned, when and how, for what kind of life, and by which people. And we have to take account of the facts that we are living in multiple societies and in a very rapidly changing world.

I want to talk under four headings: democracy, fairness, competition, interdependence.

'Democracy' means at least two things. One is a system of government, in which the rule of one-person-one-vote operates, and the minority acquiesces in the majority decision. The second is a society in which opportunities are widely open, in which talent and effort are rewarded, privilege is not excessive and compassion is exercised. When a majority prevails, neither the rich nor the poor should readily assume that their interests will be highly regarded by the majority, since both of them are, by definition, minorities.

Fairness

In our society this notion involves the view that talent and effort will be rewarded, and that there will be the same rules for all. A central question is how we are going to have, in an increasingly interdependent world, universal principles when we have such different practical circumstances (rich and poor) and different cultures?

These apparently conflicting demands for universality and particular difference can only be reconciled if you have a set of universal values, and apply them progressively with sensitivity to the different societies that are concerned. In some societies there may have to be what the Americans call 'affirmative action'. But there is an interesting controversy going on in America about how to avoid the tyranny of the majority which is a real problem for Blacks where democracy, in the governmental sense, prevails. Environmental regulations provide a good example of the need to be affirmative yet fair. There cannot be effective international action on environmental problems such as were discussed at Rio and elsewhere, if we lack universal measurements. But we also need a new form of diplomacy. There has to be a set of standards which really affects the worst Western polluters more than others. And because we can't say that the environment is a global problem and then ignore India and China, unlike things will have to be equated.

For example, whilst the Western countries agree to limit carbon dioxide emissions by all the ways talked about, and within precise timescales, Third World countries will have to take steps in the field of population control, public health, education. The issue of non-tariff barriers is another area in which not everyone can apply the same standards.

Fairness, in our culture, is linked with the idea of social cohesiveness: this is partly because of our notions of justice and compassion and the adverse consequences of a lack of social cohesion. There is a strong instinct in most societies to avoid the consequences of lack of social cohesion. But I would like to mention here the increasing strains that we are likely to encounter as a result of migration and the interdependence which promotes migration, and as a result of international competition.

Competition

If you don't have something to sell, you have no income. In a knowledge society, knowledge is one of the chief commodities that gets bought and sold. Such knowledge has to be sold in competition with others, and the traditional economics of supply and demand apply, along with other factors such as: quality, R&D, servicing, reliability and so on. These are all areas in which education has a role to play.

<u>Interdependence</u>

Some dominant trends in the world are worth noting. There is growing and spreading affluence in the world. But if affluence is spreading amongst much the larger part of the world so is the gap between the rich countries and the poor countries.

The second gap, which I take very seriously, is the increasing gap in <u>each</u> society between the rich and the poor. The difference between the maritime provinces in China and the interior, as we have all read recently, has just become enormous, leading potentially to great instability. India is absolutely transformed in the 12-15 years I have been closely associated with it. In 1977 the middle classes numbered about 40 million; whereas now the Governor of the Reserve Bank refers to a number in excess of 200 million.

Now that the Cold War is over the dominant international trend is going to concern struggles over trade. There will continue to be a struggle for a long time between liberal trade versus protectionism. The current French Prime Minister, M. Balladur recently said (I translate his words): "Can we West Europeans take it for granted that we will remain sufficient leaders in a sufficient number of sectors to survive, in the face of countries with populations infinitely larger than ours and with levels of social protection infinitely smaller. I say we should leave this to the market but only up to a certain point. What is the market? It is the law of the jungle, the law of nature. And what is civilisation? It is the struggle against nature". That regrettable statement represents the thinking of an increasing number of people in Western Europe who are conscious of figures such as the following: in 1993 the hourly labour costs in manufacturing were: for Germany $24.90, for Japan $16.90, for the US $16.40 and for Britain $12.40: for South Korea $4.90, for Hungary $1.80 and for China $0.50 (*The New York Times*, 17 April 1994). Those figures indicate much of what lies behind M. Balladur's comments.

Between 1980-1991 the value of the European Community's internal trade in manufactures rose 167% but its external exports increased by only 79%, whereas the US exports increased by 129% and Japanese by 146%.

Financial flows and technology have both escaped government control, and that matters a great deal.

Another trend concerns what I call universalism versus cultural particularism. The controversy about human rights is fundamental, and I have already said that it requires great maturity at one and the same time to hold to a set of universal principles and yet not apply them universally or evenly.

We need also to reflect on the values of our education in a context of ethnic conflict and of minority problems. One point of conflict between ethnic groups centres on the language, and language for teaching: so there are issues of who is going to control the schools, using what language and what curriculum. Also all of us who are concerned with this problem hold that the most important thing to do to ameliorate it - one can't I think resolve it - is to educate everybody. That is to say to educate the majority as well as the minority.

Another major problem concerns the population growth and migration. The phrase 'nation state' is nowadays very awkward, and in any case has only been used in the last 200 years. Nations and states have not historically been coincident and they won't be in the very near future.

A further issue is the tremendous growth in the importance of non-governmental organisations. Governments are increasingly recognising that they cannot do lots of things, and especially at grassroots levels.

Conclusions

All governments are recognising that the future of their countries is very closely bound up with education.

A paradox: as the pace of events quickens, as society gets more complicated, so education must become more basic. By 'basic education' I mean education that has continuing relevance: already much of it is out of date within ten years. Education must fundamentally be about learning to learn. If basics are as important as I am saying they are, then nobody should be allowed to miss out on them. We have to face up to raising the age of compulsory education.

Citizenship, tolerance, motivation: all are essential in a pluralist society.

We need some sticks as well as carrots. I would seriously consider linking some Social Security benefits, even pensions, to an achievement of literacy. I quite like the idea of loans and paybacks, which is not unlike the idea of conscription in wartime. When society provides the education it is reasonable to pay something back to society.

I would like also to do something about female education in

developing countries. My proposal for that is that all aid - including aid from the largest donors, such as the World Bank - should have as a condition that, say, 2% of it went to female education and must be matched by an equivalent amount from the government receiving the aid.

In drawing up our values we should try to remember that we are drawing them up for a world that is evolving very rapidly and in which we are living in several societies at once. That is a very desirable thing: living in several societies at once, being members of several groups is the best prophylactic to extreme nationalism and ethnic conflict.

Discussion

It was emphasised that the study of other societies is a valuable element in educational curricula, because almost all cultures, traditions and religions contain resources that can contribute to a cohesive society.

Basic education, however, is not a privilege but an entitlement; not in the sense that one should think of taking from society, but in the sense that it is in society's own interests to have a basically well-educated community.

70

Implicit in much present day discussion is the need for teaching teachers. Teachers must address several questions: how can we best help our successors to deal with the future? How can we educate our successors, train them, forewarn them, guard them, prepare them for these issues? What skills, capacities, frames of mind are going to be necessary? How are they to be acquired? When are they going to be acquired? How are they going to be moderated and tested? It might help to think of education not as conferring an entitlement to withdraw a finite sum from the bank, but as establishing a continually evolving frame of mind which requires us to be creative and rationally flexible throughout our lives.

It could be argued that the four headings (democracy, fairness, competition, interdependence) are not of equal importance, or not on the same level, or are even incompatible. Competition, for example, is inimical to good research, scholarship and teaching - all of which are enhanced by collaboration. Moreover, competition is an intermediate good which we take to be a means of supplying something we all want; that is to say, helping us to approach the goal of happiness.

It may even become necessary in the future to contain international competitiveness if it endangers people's lifestyles; and yet such international control might prove generally unacceptable as long as there are desperately poor countries in the world.

In this context, it is instructive to consider the four categories in a South African educational system. Those who have been excluded for 50-60 years from the established set of values or symbols of excellence, now regard them as illegitimate. The construction of an alternative agenda of entitlement, which the ANC and other parties are involved with, might overtly undermine the symbols of excellence, and generate a new range of problems.

Strengths and Weaknesses of Education in the Western Pacific

Masao Kunihiro

As some of you may know, in Japan, and in much of the rest of what now is known as East Asia, a public speaker is expected (almost obligated) to begin a public presentation with a few apologies, whereas in your part of the world, one is expected to begin with a few jokes or humorous stories. As I am Japanese through and through, I will begin with a couple of excuses.

My first apology refers to my English. While many of my colleagues here are native speakers of impeccable English, mine is "peccable with a Japanese accent". In fact, expressing myself in English leaves me with the taste of "scratching the itchy spots from above the shoe" (as we say in Chinese and consequently in Japanese too). Or, should I say I feel as if I were an acrobat trying to walk a tight rope without falling off the wire as I speak to you in English - a language I was not born speaking.

My second apology pertains to the fact I will have to hold in abeyance until the question time, the subject of informal education - the protean question which issues from parents, peers, churches, temples, Boy Scout leaders, judo instructors, and last but never least, television tubes which Senator Fulbright, of the Fulbright

Exchange Program fame, referred to as "that idiot box".

Thirdly, I am <u>not</u>, by any stretch of semantic generosity, an expert either in pedagogy or sociology of knowledge. However, I have been associated with several universities as a teacher, and have published several books pertaining to education in the broad sense of the term, including translations into Japanese of David Riesman's *The Academic Revolution*, Herbert Passin's *Society and Education in Japan*, and Benjamin Duke's *The Japanese School*. This goes to prove that I am interested in education as a human endeavour in general, and education in Japan in particular. Besides, I have been associated with the educational end of NHK television which is the Japanese counterpart of the BBC. I also sat on the Education Committee in the Upper House for a total of four years, and I am unhappy to report to you that while in 1975, 12.2% of the state budget (as opposed to 7.7% in 1970) was earmarked for education, the ratio went down to a mere 7.2% this year - a yardstick with which to gauge the degree of national commitment to education. Since I sit also on the Budget Committee I feel personally responsible and guilty for this measurable decline in our educational commitment.

Fourthly, as I talk about the Nurture of the Young and deal with the way in which our cultures and societies train the minds and sensibilities of our young people in East Asia, my remarks will be more or less confined to Japan. I feel somewhat confident in dealing with China because of my not really short acquaintance with its letters and traditions, augmented by my rather frequent visits there. I am totally ill equipped to discuss in any educational treatise the other no less important players in our part of the world - two Koreas and Vietnam.

In this connection, let me spend some time introducing the concept of the Sinitic Confucian Culture Area which is gaining a wider currency as a hypothesis to account for the explosive growth now being made by the 'Four Little Dragons' and by China itself in the economic, industrial and social arenas.

To cite one example, by way of illustration: The World Bank, in April last year, made a prediction that by 2002 the combined GDPs of China, Taiwan and Hong Kong, at 9.8 trillion dollars, will exceed that of the U.S. at 9.7 trillion and Japan at 4.9 trillion dollars. Undersecretary Summers of the U.S. Treasury Department went on to say that by 2020 the GDP of China alone will exceed the combined GDPs of the U.S. and Japan. Of course, there are more cautious souls within China itself, including my long-time friend Professor Mouhong, Vice Chairman of the Chinese Association of Asian and African Studies, who in a recently held symposium in

Beijing, openly challenged a too rosy view of the Asia Era itself and of China's role in it. He warned that it is somewhat self-deceiving if such terms as 'golden chances' and 'bright prospects' usher in further undue propaganda of imaginary future glory which might fuel rashness. He declared "I am not ignoring opportunities but we have to look reality in the face". Similarly, Professor F. Zhaoku, Vice Director of the Institute of Japanese Studies of the Chinese Academy of Social Sciences warned against "bubble economies" in the region, stating that the 21st century might provide more challenges than opportunities for China.

Despite these expressions of caution and cool-headedness in China itself, attempts have been made to explain the tremendous economic growth which appears to be confined to East Asia - not only from the perspective of political, civil and industrial structure but also in terms of socio-cultural traits and religious-philosophical traditions of the region, to identify the possible major cause of such enormous economic and social progress.

The late Herman Kahn, a noted American mathematician-turned-strategist-futurologist, startled the world, including the Japanese themselves, with the prediction of over 30 years ago that "the 21st Century may well belong to Japan", if certain conditions were met. His advocacy of the concept of the Confucian Culture

Area was to be elaborated upon by a group of highly respected scholars such as Chalmers Johnson of the University of California in San Diego, Lucian Pie of the MIT, Ronald Dore of the Imperial College of London and L. Vandermeersch of the University of Paris. All of them are first rate scholars and are well versed in languages and cultures of East Asia.

In the face of the enormous strides now being made in much of East Asia and among the so-called Asian NIES, this concept began to enjoy an increasingly wider currency in somewhat the same fashion as the revered thesis of Max Weber, who sought a key to explain the formation of capitalism in Protestant, more specifically Puritan, Europe. It is ironical that while Max Weber down-graded the Confucian tradition as a possible stumbling block in the genesis of capitalism in the Far East, these latter day saints with a good background and expertise in East Asian languages and cultures, hit upon the Confucian tradition as a plausible explanation of why those parts of Asia in the Sinitic Confucian Culture area are doing so well in economic and industrial development, and in high levels of social cohesiveness and order.

Two recent books setting out such views have been published, the first in the US and the second in Australia: *East Asian Region: Confucian Heritage and Its Modern Adaptation* and

The Confucian Renaissance: Origins of Asia's Economic Development.

Here, I am not without some deep-felt emotions because when Robert Bellah, the celebrated American sociologist came up with his immortal *Tokugawa Religion* as an application of the Max Weber theory to Japan and its rapid industrial modernization, non-protestant, non-Western Japan was singled out to test the Weberian theory and no-one ever imagined that the day might come so soon when the whole of East Asia received a similar scrutiny. Remember that, with an amazing insight to "look into the seeds of time" as Shakespeare put it, Bellah wrote his thesis as early as 1959. What he found was a semi-scholarly yet basically very pragmatic and merchant-class orientated movement of Shingaku, initiated by Ishida Baigan (1685-1744), which was an amalgam of teachings of Shintoism, Buddhism and Confucianism - a very appropriate combination in Japan, a land of syncretism. Now back at Princeton, Bellah is concentrating on the Moslem tradition and its bearings upon the process of industrialization (or lack of it) in the Near and Middle East. I wish him well, because it is obviously a formidable, yet extremely timely, task.

There are four salient characteristics of Confucianism relevant to our interest in the Nurture of the Young, according to

Ronald Dore's 1989 speech "Confucianism, Economic Growth and Social Development". First: dutifulness to a larger collectivity, as opposed to individual rights to the pursuit of happiness. Second: the proclivity toward accepting a system of hierarchy. Third: special roles assigned to elites who are highly educated; those with knowledge are entitled to moral authority to rule. Fourth: rationality. Professor De Bary of Columbia University has maintained that, popular views of Confucianism as authoritarian to the contrary, a case can readily be made for both Liberalism and Democracy within the Confucian tradition.

On the third point, (like the Prussians from whom we borrowed heavily in the early Meiji years) Confucianism identified the goals of education with the goals of the state, whilst safeguarding opportunities for individual self-improvement and advancement. In emphasizing the need for merit, rather than rank, education assumed a major role, as Confucius himself insisted in his *Analects*. His teachings invoked and enhanced the very rigorous tradition of competition in education as a preparation for high societal position, and which contributed to the unique system of mandarin bureaucracy which for over 2000 years ruled China.

So, perhaps, the emphasis traditionally placed upon education as a means of self-improvement and as an avenue for one's promotion from the ranks up the hierarchy, may explain the avid enthusiasm for education observable even among the masses in the Confucian Culture Area, and may in turn account for the rapid process of modernisation now being experienced in the East Asian region as a whole.

Now about Japan.

As a non-Aristotelian nurtured in the tradition where something is and is not at the same time in a mutually permeable way, where something is fair and foul simultaneously, where mutual exclusivity or the digital yes-or-no, zero-or-one dichotomy is not the name of the game, I am both positive and negative about education in Japan. I am cognizant of both strengths and weaknesses, both successes and failures, and will try to put both of them in some sort of perspective.

I am well aware that Japanese schools have been widely and sometimes even wildly admired, as in the case of former U.S. Education Secretary Bennet who lauded to the skies the test-coaching cram schools of Japan which to me are nothing but a scourge. Japanese schools are admired for their success in instilling high levels of literacy and numeracy in the population at large. The Japanese have indeed achieved almost universal literacy, second only to Finland (UNESCO data) at 97% or so, with the U.S. and the U.K. lagging somewhat behind.

Of course, I am acutely aware of the intricacy of the notion of literacy. There are various definitions of literacy, with wide-ranging ramifications especially in multi-racial, multi-lingual cultures of the world. There is another emerging problem of functional illiteracy, and I have to confess I am totally illiterate in computer or mathematical language. Even during the mid-Tokugawa period in the early 19th Century, and on the most conservative estimates, Japan approached 50% literacy among boys and 20% or so among girls.

Apart from over 230 schools established and maintained by different fiefs, for the training of their Samurai retainers, the late 18th century witnessed the birth of what we called Terakoya, or temple schools, where instructions were given to humble folk in reading, writing, and arithmetic, as well as practical wisdom to increase men's efficiency in their hereditary occupations. It is noteworthy that, despite their name, most of the instructions given were secular in nature, with very little theological or religious indoctrination.

By 1850, the number of such temple schools had reached

almost 6,000, and by the Meiji Restoration of 1868, the number had almost doubled to 12,000. In what is now known as Tokyo, there were well over 1200 such schools enjoying a thriving business. With a total Japanese population of less than 25 million, the prosperity of so numerous institutions of primary and secondary learning was a spectacular phenomenon. As a corollary to formal education, in 1710 Japan already had 600 publishers and booksellers: in 1809, 656 lending libraries were doing business in Tokyo alone. In 1837, barely one British child in four or five entered a school, and I recall the poor level of mass education referred to in Dickensian novels, alongside such world famed institutions of higher learning as Oxford and Cambridge, to say nothing of the great Scottish institutions. The discrepancy was enormous in Britain, while Japan tended to be a bit more egalitarian in dispensation of knowledge and learning.

So, as Japan opened its doors to the rest of the world, she had met some of the basic requirements for the process of 'modernisation' that ensued: in terms of basic literacy and numeracy; in terms of achievement orientation at the grass roots level; in terms of a deeply inculcated sense of duty and obligation towards the immediate community as well as the larger society. When the Meiji oligarchy in 1872 advocated that "there shall be no uneducated families in a community and no unlettered members in a family" it was a bold policy orientation, yet all the ingredients were available.

As regards numeracy, in several international UNESCO mathematics tests, Japanese youngsters proved to be the best in the world, although Korean and Chinese students, including Taiwanese and those from Hong Kong, are faring very well recently.

Now I have to tell you that the good news stops here - all too abruptly.

If we have been successful in instilling high levels of literacy and numeracy, we have to ask ourselves if we have been reasonably (if not equally) successful in qualitative terms in encouraging the students to develop the kind of imagination to cope with ailments peculiar to post-industrial cultures: anomie, alienation, cultural entropy, and most urgently, ecological disaster? Likewise, if we have been moderately successful in inculcating in our students the traditional values of the culture, how successful have we been in inducing them to manage to test those values against the swiftly changing necessities of life?

And what about internationalization or globalization which is on everybody's lips in today's Japan? The need to make allowances for greater diversity and pluralism in an otherwise highly monolingual, monoracial, endogamous Japan is piously debated. However, we have again to ask ourselves if we have been at all successful in encouraging our students to go beyond the parochial and often exclusionistic barriers of sovereign nation states in their perception and awareness, and to think in broader and perhaps in ecological, Spaceship Earth, terms appropriate to the progressively 'annihilated distance' (Toynbee) and rapidly 'shrunken space' (Reischauer) of our time. The system seems to many overseas observers and Japanese, including ex-Education Minister Michio Nagai (a noted educationalist with a broad offshore background), to be on the brink of serious trouble, with cut-throat competition to prestigious schools, conflict over textbook censorship by the government, and educational institutions insulated from the larger society. Is this good?

At the risk of self-flagellation, I have to answer all these questions more in the negative than in the affirmative.

On the ecological front, a UNEP study several years ago showed Japanese youngsters to be the least concerned over the environment, and the least willing to help those individuals and organizations engaged valiantly in the prevention of further environmental degradation.

This is in a country which has claimed to be actively orientated toward symbiosis, toward man with nature in place of man against nature, where love of Nature has been held to be a cardinal virtue and a characteristic of the culture.

Similarly, the degree of ignorance on the part of the young about the legacy of the former imperial, militaristic Japan, especially in its relations to the rest of Asia, is simply appalling. Perhaps reflecting a national proclivity towards historical amnesia, Japanese youngsters are actively not taught about the atrocities inflicted on the Chinese by the one-million strong Japanese invading forces. (Only 6 million Jews were massacred, while we were responsible for the deaths of 12 million Chinese, even by a conservative estimate.) An expert in contemporary history was recently asked by a serious university student in Tokyo if Japan had been at war with the United States, and, if so, which side had won. The student was obviously fed on television and newspaper commentaries on the weak dollar and the strong yen, and American tendencies to be defensive in economic and trade matters. Disturbingly enough, many youngsters were mesmerized by the 'Japan as No. 1 Syndrome' (the term I coined after Harvard Professor Ezra Vogel's *Japan as Number One*).

So something is definitely rotten with the state of education in Japan despite its facade of success. We have been less than successful in preparing our youngsters for the requirements of further globalization.

On a somewhat different level, the youngsters today appear to be long on hedonism and short on the kind of Shinto-Confucian-Buddhist work ethic which so far accounts for Japan's success. Even university students in more than middling institutions don't work half as hard as at overseas institutions. The university typically is referred to as a "leisure-land", and students while away at least the first two or three years until such a time as employment opportunities begin to loom large in their 3rd or 4th year.

Let me try to shed some light on the less positive sides to the academic picture. Our youngsters do well in mathematics tests, and the level of mathematics instruction in our primary and secondary education is high. We have three recipients of the very coveted Fields Prize, given every four years, unlike the annual Nobel Prizes. When I asked the first Japanese Fields winner, Professor Kunihiko Kodaira if the level of mathematics we boast of was really first rate in the world, he replied: Yes, first rate as far as finding solutions to existing questions is concerned, but never first rate when it comes to creating new, unprecedented questions.

Now that all of us in the world, particularly in the developed world (what an effrontery for us to make such claims), lack existing textbook answers to problems of an unprecedented nature all across the spectrum of human existence, what counts is the ability to think the unthinkable, to imagine the unimaginable. But Professor Kodaira seems to believe that we in Japan are sadly lacking in this kind of creative and innovative ingenuity.

This failing emerges more sharply when we realise that Japan has produced only 5 Nobel laureates in the natural sciences, when Britain has 64, Germany 60, France 24, Russia 10, Italy 7, to say nothing of the U.S. who has 156 scientists on the Nobel list.

Paucity of Nobel winners in Japan totally incommensurate with its economic, industrial, academic and educational might, appears to be illustrative of our inadequacies in basic, pure research if not product-related, merchandise-orientated applied research. Like the author of *The Japanese School*, I can hardly be too sanguine about the future of Japan which, like it or not, will have to be drawn to more acute global competition in the not too remote future.

Here, I have to make a confession that even the very best institutions of higher learning, which should act as the bastion of basic research, are seriously handicapped in funding and also in the quality of students. The preponderance of profit-related applied research by companies over pure, basic research is becoming increasingly apparent, with universities begging the companies to distribute some share of their product-related research, weakening still further the base for basic research. Also, it is an open secret that Japanese university students need to study very little, in comparison with students in the best British and American institutions.

Here, Ronald Dore's distinction between education and qualifications can be a very useful tool. To him, education involves changing people: it depends on awakening and sustaining by a continuous process of partial satisfaction and further stimulation, curiosity and the desire for self-development, the desire to understand, the desire to achieve, and the desire to master. Qualification, on the other hand, is merely "instrumental":

> the passive absorption of ready-made answers in order to become qualified, certified, and entitled to a job, a salary and social status. Education results from the desire to learn, qualification results from the desire to be certified as having learnt. Education is a learning as an end itself, or as a means to action; qualification is the merely

instrumental use of learning, not to do, but just to
be.

(Education in Tokugawa Japan)

This is a serious and stern indictment of the state of education in Japan by a highly erudite yet compassionate observer. Students are interested only in being on the automatic escalator that guarantees their post-graduation jobs and careers. It is their admission to best universities that counts to employers, who begin to recruit even sophomores - "cutting the rice green", they say. No wonder 75%-80% of a recent freshman class at Tokyo University spent at least one year in 'cram school' whose only purpose is to coach youngsters to learn all the 'inert facts' (in the parlance of the great philosopher Alfred North Whitehead) in preparation, and only in preparation, for the entrance examination which is known as examination hell. Internalization of these 'inert' facts is totally out of the question; we have only "garbage in, garbage out".

In the typical Japanese classroom, the stifling of animated spontaneity among students and between teachers and students, except at kindergarten and primary school levels, is the rule which discourages non-Japanese teachers and/or returnees from overseas. The sticks that stand out, as we say, are nailed down. By actively asking questions or by trying to debate issues, students tend to make themselves persona non grata, and are alienated as nuisances not just by their peers but even by their teachers as well. Children who are ambitious, in the sense of getting to the best schools, or are offspring of ambitious parents, quite literally lose their youth, from about 12 years on, until they enter a university. Many of these youngsters are burnt-out by the time they reach a university, and Professor Koji Nakanishi, the most likely candidate for the Nobel Prize for Chemistry, argues that the university entrance examination is the major culprit and should be completely and finally abolished. The author of *The Japanese School,* Professor Duke, argues that the effort to deposit more information faster in Japanese schools than in their American counterparts simply deprives the youngsters of the will to learn on their own initiative, and prematurely burns out the individual initiative to learn. He advocates that the level of instruction in terms of inert facts in high school should be lowered, so that the students will have a reservoir of energy and initiative not totally consumed by the time they get into college.

For a long time, Japan has been known as a society with a minimum of anti-intellectualism. When Professor & Mrs. David Riesman visited Japan for the first time in 1960 as people-seers (instead of sight-seers as he put it), they were impressed with the apparent lack of anti-intellectualism in Japanese society. They experienced the jam-packed trains during rush-hours in Tokyo, and their eyes really popped out when they noticed many a commuter reading serious authors such as Sartre, Marx and Lord Keynes, while precariously hanging on to straps. He wondered if the difficulty of acquiring a working knowledge of several thousand Chinese characters guarded against anti-intellectualism: after all the investment one has made in time, energy, money etc., in acquiring enough Chinese ideograms, one may as well treat it preciously rather than casually.

We should perhaps ask ourselves whether quantity and quality can be pursued simultaneously in education? To put it rather radically, is democratic education doomed to mediocrity? Can excellence be an achievable goal in mass education? Since 1840 when Alexis de Tocquville wrote of his concern that mass democracy might lead to a culture of mediocrity, this has been a perennial theme in any serious debate on public education and democracy in the US and, though to a lesser extent, in Japan also.

It seems that we will have to face up to this big question sooner or later (or perhaps sooner than later) in Japan. The tyranny of the majority is quite possible in a Japan which is becoming a democracy of the masses at an ever increasing speed and on a progressively larger scale. Can we aim at excellence and quantity at the same time? Can we kill two birds with a single stone? On this inquisitive note, let me bring my rambling, fugitive remarks to a close by thanking you for your kind attention.

LIST OF PARTICIPANTS

ALEXANDER, Sir Kenneth Chancellor, University of Aberdeen

CAMPS, Senator Victoria Senator of the Spanish Parliament; former Professor, Universitat Autonoma de Barcelona

CASSELS, Sir John Director, National Commission on Education

CLYDE, The Hon. Lord Senator of the College of Justice, Edinburgh

COWARD, Professor Harold Director, Centre for Studies in Religion & Society, University of Victoria, British Columbia

CUBIE, Mr. Andrew Senior Partner, Fyfe Ireland, WS

DALYELL, Mr. Tam Member of Parliament for Linlithgow

ELLIOT, Sir Gerald Chairman, Prince's Scottish Youth Business Trust; Former Chairman, Christian Salvesen PLC; Scottish Opera; Scottish Arts Council

FRASER, Sir William Principal & Vice Chancellor, University of Glasgow

HARDING, Professor Dennis Abercromby Professor of Archaeology, University of Edinburgh

HOWIE, Professor John Regius Professor of Mathematics, University of St. Andrews

IZZO, Dr. Giancarlo Consul General of Italy, Edinburgh

JONES, Professor Peter Director, Institute for Advanced Studies in the Humanities, University of Edinburgh

KANEKO, Mr. Yoshikazu Consul General of Japan, Edinburgh

KING, Professor Kenneth Department of Education, University of Edinburgh

KUNIHIRO, Senator Masao House of Councillors, Tokyo

McBAIN, Mr. Barclay Education Correspondent, The Herald

MILLER, Professor Andrew Vice Principal, University of Edinburgh

POWNEY, Ms Janet Programme Manager, The Scottish Council for Research in Education

RICHARDSON, Professor John Provost, Arts, Divinity and Music, University of Edinburgh

RISK, Sir Thomas Former Governor of the Bank of Scotland

RUSSELL, Sir Mark Former H.M. Ambassador to Turkey

SERRACINO-INGLOTT, Rev. Prof. Peter Rector, University of Malta

SHAW, Professor Jack Chairman, Scottish Higher Education Funding Council

THOMSON, Sir John Former UK Permanent Representative to the United Nations